DATE		
OCT 22 1984	NOV 2 4 1988	
DEC 25 1986	MAY 3 0 1999	
MAR 10 1987	MAY 2 0 1988	
MAY 5 1987	MAR 2 6 2003	
JAN 1 0 1989		
DEC 0 7 1993		
MAY 1 2 1995		
AUG 3 1 1996		
MAY 3 0 1997		

WITHDRAWN

Wildlife on the African Grasslands

Wildlife on the

Messner Books by Mary Adrian
WILDLIFE ON THE AFRICAN GRASSLANDS
WILDLIFE IN THE ANTARCTIC

99.0967
Adr

$7.95
14303

African Grasslands

by Mary Adrian
Illustrated by Bette J. Davis

Julian Messner New York

Copyright © 1979 by Mary Adrian
Illustrations Copyright © 1979 by Bette J. Davis
All rights reserved including the right of
reproduction in whole or in part in any form.
Published by Julian Messner, a Simon and Schuster
Division of Gulf & Western Corporation, Simon &
Schuster Building, 1230 Avenue of the Americas,
New York, N.Y. 10020.

Manufactured in the United States of America

Design by Alex D'Amato

Library of Congress Cataloging in Publication Data

Adrian, Mary, 1908–
  Wildlife on the African grasslands.

  SUMMARY: Describes the varied animal life of the
African grasslands, focusing on the lion, leopard,
cheetah, and zebra. Also describes efforts to protect
increasingly scarce African wildlife.
  Includes index.
  1. Grassland fauna—Africa—Juvenile literature.
2. Zoology—Africa—Juvenile literature. [1. Grassland
animals—Africa. 2. Zoology—Africa] I. Davis,
Bette J. II. Title.
QL336.A4   599′.0967   79-994
ISBN 0-671-32999-5

Contents

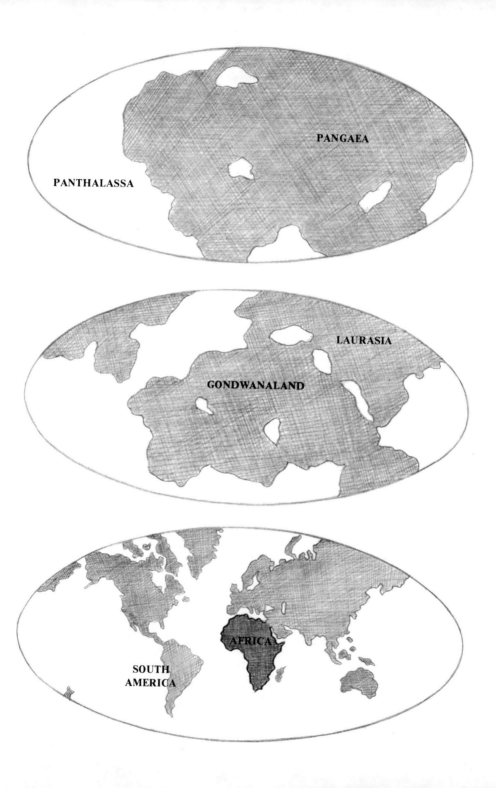

1 · Africa

Many hundreds of millions of years ago, there were no continents as they are today. Instead, there was only one gigantic landmass. Geologists call the landmass Pangaea, which means many lands. It was surrounded by one ocean, Panthalassa, which means many seas.

Two hundred million years ago, Pangaea split into two huge landmasses. One was the northern part which is known as Laurasia. The other was the southern part called Gondwanaland. The split was caused by the earth's shifting crust which is made up of gigantic plates that move slowly.

Gondwanaland and Laurasia did not remain two large landmasses. The earth's plates kept moving, much like huge ice floes pushing about on a frozen sea. As a result, Gondwanaland and Laurasia gradually split into other, smaller landmasses. Those that split off from Gondwanaland drifted apart. After many millions of years they became the present-day continents of Africa, South America, Australia, Antarctica and the subcontinent of India.

About a million years ago, glaciers of a great Ice Age slowly pushed down from the north, and the wild animals moved southward. Some did not survive. Others crossed land bridges that connected one continent with another, and moved on to Africa where the grasslands made perfect living places because of the warm climate, plenty of rainfall and food.

The black rhinoceros that lives in Africa today is a reminder of the very large animals that once roamed the African grasslands. In fact, it is a "living fossil" since it looks very much like its prehistoric ancestors that have been found in fossil remains.

Fossils are the hard parts of plants and animals, such as bones, shells and branches. They can also be a record of life such as footprints. All are preserved in the rocks by natural processes.

Fossil records also show that just a few thousand years ago in Africa, there were giant baboons and hippopotamuses twice the size of these present-day animals.

There is something else about the African grasslands. It was here that fossil skeletons of the oldest humans were discovered.

Most of Africa is a giant plateau, a raised section of land. The grasslands cover almost half of its surface. There

University School
Media Center

are three main grasslands. One of them lies between the Sahara desert in the north and the rain forests in the south, near the equator. The other two are in eastern and southern Africa. Many parts of the African grasslands are rolling plains. These are covered by tall grasses where the rainfall is high, and short grasses where the rainfall is low.

Some of the grasslands have widely spaced trees and shrubs. Others have no trees except along the banks of some streams. Because of the changing vegetation and the differing amounts of rainfall, the kinds and numbers of animals vary from place to place.

Many grassland animals eat mostly grass. These are the grazers. They include antelope, zebras and buffaloes.

Animals that feed on grass as well as on other plants are known as browsers. They are the elephants, giraffes and black rhinoceroses.

Others, such as hippopotamuses, warthogs, baboons, and many smaller kinds of animals, eat very little or no grass. But they do eat the bark, twigs, leaves, fruits, nuts and roots of trees and plants.

The meat-eating animals of the grasslands are the lions, leopards, cheetahs, hyenas and wild dogs. They are called predators because they feed on the plant-eating animals.

2 · The Pride of Lions

It was June, the beginning of the dry summer season on the grasslands of eastern Africa. The sun's hot rays were turning the tall grasses a golden yellow. The flowers had lost their freshness from the heat. But the leaves of the umbrella-shaped acacia trees were still green, and birds flitted among the branches.

Under one of the trees, a pride of lions rested in the shade. Lions like the company of other lions. Of the several different kinds of cats, they are the only ones that live in family groups. Some prides are large, others are small.

This pride was made up of a male lion, two females, and five cubs. The male lion weighed 400 pounds. His mane of tan-colored hair hung around his neck like a huge collar. Each of the two lionesses was 100 pounds lighter and did not have a shaggy mane. The cubs—three males and two females—were almost four months old. They still had their brown baby spots, and they liked to play.

This afternoon they wrestled in the grass. Then standing up, they batted each other with their paws and mouthed each other, but they did not bite. One cub left his companions, and pounced on the black tassel of hair at the end of his mother's tail. He held it between his paws, shook it, and bit it.

The lioness pulled her tail away from the cub. He grabbed it again. Growling in anger, she arose and slapped him with her big paw. He cringed and cried pitifully, but a few moments later he was chasing the other cubs around the acacia tree.

The lioness lay down and watched a giraffe browse on an acacia tree nearby. The giraffe sensed that the lioness would not attack because she was not hungry. No danger was in sight.

From its towering height of seventeen feet, the giraffe

looked out across the grasslands, and continued stripping leaves from the tree with its eighteen-inch tongue. The thorns on the branches were sharp, but the giraffe's thick, gummy saliva protected its mouth. His lower jaw went round and round as he chewed the leaves.

Not far from the giraffe, a small herd of zebras were grazing. They were biting off the tall grasses and eating them. No doubt, they knew that the lion and lionesses were resting because they did not raise their heads to look for danger. Then, too, the giraffe was close by and would warn them of an approaching enemy by galloping away.

A short while later the lionesses took a nap. At sundown they were awakened by the roaring of the lion. His huge head moved up and down as he uttered deep, moaning calls that ended with low grunts. He was warning other lions to stay out of the pride's hunting grounds.

When the twilight shadows crept over the grasslands, and no intruder had come into his territory, the lion seemed satisfied. But he was hungry and moved about restlessly.

The cubs also wanted food. They had lived on their mother's milk the first two months of their lives, and now they were eating fresh meat. One cub miaowed that he was hungry, and was quickly joined by a chorus from his brothers and sisters.

The lionesses finally paid attention to their cries. After making the cubs bed down in a thicket where a predator

could not easily see them, they set out together on a hunting trip.

The male lion went along. Sometimes a lion joins in a hunt and helps the lionesses to attack prey for food. If he is very hungry, he will kill an animal by himself. But this night, the lion wanted the lionesses to do the hunting.

The three of them moved along single file through the tall grasses without making a sound. No moon shone in the sky to light their way, but their gold-colored eyes were made for seeing in the dark. Besides, the night was the best time to sneak up on an animal and kill it.

Soon the lionesses fanned out. They crouched low in the grass a short distance from each other and, switching their tails from side to side, waited for their prey. The lion was a stone's throw away, also hidden from sight.

A short while later, there was a noise in the brush close by. The lionesses pricked up their ears and listened carefully. In a few moments, they saw a large waterbuck antelope with long spreading horns standing a few yards away.

Slowly the animal started walking in the direction of the hidden lionesses. As it stopped and sniffed the air for a danger scent, one lioness, her belly to the ground, snaked toward the antelope. The other lioness also moved forward.

Just then the waterbuck saw the second lioness. Frantic, it changed direction and ran in a fast gallop toward the other lioness. Quick as a flash, she reached up and grabbed the large antelope with both of her huge paws. She slammed it down to the ground and clamped its muzzle shut with her teeth. The second lioness rushed in and killed the waterbuck.

The male lion immediately bounded up and began to eat, while one lioness went back to get the waiting cubs. She roared softly, and they came running toward her. They followed her to the kill, but the lion shoved them aside. He wanted his share first. He ate until his belly was so plump that it almost dragged along the ground.

The lionesses were next. After they had eaten their fill,
they allowed the cubs to have their share. The cubs tore at
the meat and ate so much that their bellies bulged like little
melons. But they managed to follow their parents back to
the acacia tree.

As soon as the pride of lions were asleep, six spotted hyenas, drawn by their sharp sense of smell, began to circle the leftovers of the kill. Hyenas are large dog-like animals and are predators, like the lions. But they live and usually hunt their prey in packs. They are also scavengers, and eat the remains of dead animals that otherwise would decay and spread disease on the grasslands.

The hyenas lost no time feeding on the waterbuck carcass. They even crushed and broke some of the bones

with their powerful jaws and sharp teeth. Then they moved
along in a rolling gait much like that of a camel. They were
patrolling their territory for trespassers. Not a star blinked in
the sky, but the hyenas, like their distant relatives, the cats,
had no trouble seeing in the dark.

After covering more of their feeding grounds, they
stopped at their boundary lines and sprayed fresh urine on
tufts of grass, rocks and trees to warn other packs of hyenas
to stay away.

Around midnight, the hyenas spotted a stranger on their territory. He was a young hyena who had not heeded the no trespassing signs. The whole pack immediately chased after him, their high-pitched howls sounding like laughing cries.

As they caught up with the trespasser, they snapped at his rump and his rear legs. They sent him, screaming and bleeding, to the edge of their boundary lines. Then they walked back and, with eyes shining like big yellow dots in the darkness, looked for more trespassers.

3 · The Leopard

Several days later, the pride of lions moved to another part of the grasslands. They were enjoying the early morning sun on a ledge that was part of a small mound of large rocks. The cubs were lying near their mother, but they got up when another lioness and her two three-months-old cubs arrived. After the lionesses had greeted each other by licking and rubbing cheeks, all the cubs began to play among the rocks.

Before long, a vulture circled overhead and alighted in the grass not far from the rock mound. It was a large bird and, like the hyena, a scavenger. As the vulture began eating the remains of a dead animal, it was joined by another vulture. Later they were chased away by a golden jackal, a medium-size animal with a musky odor. Being another member of nature's clean-up crew, the jackal ate well of the rotting carcass and then buried it.

A short distance away, a herd of zebras were grazing. They looked up at an approaching parade of four elephants. Each one weighed about six tons. They were the zebras' friends. So the zebras just watched the elephants shuffle along with a white cattle egret perched on each of their backs.

The birds seemed to be enjoying the ride, but they were also eating the insects that the elephants stirred up in the grass. At the same time, the egrets were acting as guards. Elephants have poor vision, but egrets have sharp eyes. They were watching for the elephants' enemies—humans with guns. This relationship between elephants and cattle egrets helping each other is called symbiosis.

At the moment the coast was clear, so the egrets did not fly up in alarm, and the elephants stopped to eat. Elephants are the largest land animals on earth, and they are always hungry. A full-grown elephant eats about 500 pounds of vegetation a day.

Using their long trunks, the elephants swept large amounts of grass into their eager mouths. They ground it up with their huge teeth and swallowed it. As they continued eating, their stomachs rumbled noisely. Still hungry, they reached high with their trunks and ate the choicest leaves and small branches on the acacia trees.

One elephant pushed against the trunk of the largest tree with his massive forehead and tusks. He rocked it three times. Then, with a mighty heave, he sent the tree crashing to the ground and had a good meal.

When the morning sun rose higher in the sky, the elephants were still feeding. But soon the sun's scorching rays sent them to shade under the trees. To keep cool, the elephants circulated the air by flapping their huge ears like fans.

Later in the day, they ate more grass, leaves, twigs and bark. They also wandered several miles and, by nightfall, they came into the hunting grounds of a leopard.

He was a handsome cat, smaller than the lion, but stronger, even though he weighed only 100 pounds. The leopard had left his mate some time before their cubs were born, and he was living alone in his territory. Leopards do not form prides as the lions do. Both male and female hunt alone all their lives. They pair off only during the mating season.

Every morning the leopard went to some trees on his boundary lines, scratched on them and wiped his face against the leaves and bark. Then he sprayed urine on them. This is the way he marks his territory, warning other leopards to keep clear of his feeding area.

After that he climbed a large acacia tree and dozed on a thick branch. His tan coat with large black, round rosettes blended with the sunlight peeping between the leaves.

This night, the leopard was still on his high perch. He could hear crickets chirping in the high grass below and a frog croaking in a pool nearby. An owl also called, loud and clear, from one of the trees. A short while later it left its perch, swooped down and caught a mouse in its talons and killed it. With a flap of wings, the owl flew silently back to the tree and had a meal.

The leopard flicked his long tail that hung over the branch of his perch. He was getting ready to hunt now. He moved to the tree trunk, dug his razor-sharp claws into the bark and climbed down, headfirst, into the high grass below.

He walked along a well-worn trail without making a sound, since his feet, like those of all leopards, were heavily cushioned with noise-muffling pads.

Listening and watching, the leopard kept moving along in the moonlight. He came to a stream and started following its banks, when suddenly he saw a duiker—one of the small African antelopes. Its coat of light brown short fur was longer on its rump, and its horns were like two small spikes. The duiker was grazing apart from the others in its herd, and did not sense danger because of the wind direction.

The leopard crouched low in the grass and then wriggled forward, silently as a shadow. He drew closer and closer to his prey. The duiker kept on eating. The leopard pounced and struck out with his thick forepaw. He brought the antelope crashing to the ground and killed it quickly.

Hold the dead duiker by the neck in his mouth and straddling it between his front legs, the leopard headed for a tree. There his kill would be safe from plundering scavengers such as jackals and hyenas that often steal another animal's kill.

Slowly the leopard kept moving. Suddenly he heard a lion growl. A large male was only a stone's throw away. Using all his strength, the leopard hurried toward a sturdy tree trunk. He reached it a few moments before the lion.

Up, up, up he climbed almost to the top where he anchored the body of the duiker between two branches. Then he looked down. The lion was coming up to the tree.

As he drew closer, the leopard climbed down the far side of the tree and took off.

The lion pulled and tugged at the dead duiker, but he could not budge it. Finally he tore it into two pieces and descended with the hindquarters in his mouth.

Later, the leopard returned to the tree and started eating the other half of his kill. But it was too much to finish in one night, so he ate the rest the next night.

4 · The Cheetah

August had come to the African grasslands with no rain in sight. The leaves of many shrubs and trees looked wilted from the heat. And haze, like a see-through curtain, hung in the air. But the rivers, streams and water holes on the grasslands had not dried up as yet, so many animals still lingered.

Zebras and different kinds of antelope nibbled dried grass among the acacia trees. Elephants and giraffes reached for leaves near the top of trees for their food. And a female warthog moved through the tall grass. Her family of four piglets trailed behind her in single file, their brush-tipped tails held upright like hers.

Soon the warthog family came to patches of short grass that had been trampled by a hippopotamus. The piglets waited while their mother dropped to her knees and snipped off grass with her sharp teeth and ate it. Then, catching the scent of a hyena, she warned her young ones and they raced to their large burrow near a thicket. Down into the hole they went, one by one, with the mother backing in last.

University School
Media Center

The hyena rushed up and peered inside the burrow. The warthog snorted, ready to attack. But the hyena drew back and trotted off to look for easier prey.

Later, the warthog took her family on another outing. She led them around a herd of huge black buffaloes that were grazing. Then they went by a small herd of antelope that were also grazing near a long-legged secretary bird. The bird was walking through the grass, nodding her head backward and forward like a hen. She made a quick dart to snatch an insect in her beak and ate it. Then she stamped the ground rapidly to disturb more prey.

But instead of scaring out insects, the sound startled a snake. It was a deadly puff adder. It slithered through the grass a few yards away, and the secretary bird raced after it. As she came closer, the snake coiled and raised its head, ready to strike. It's bite would mean instant death.

The secretary bird darted quickly to one side. Then she pounced on the snake with her powerful feet, pinning it to the ground. She grabbed its head in her beak.

The snake struggled to get free. It wriggled every which way. The secretary bird would not let go. Flapping her wings, she carried her victim into the air and then dropped it on a rock. The puff adder lay there, dead. The secretary bird landed and then began eating the snake.

All this while the warthog and her four piglets had watched the kill. Now she moved along with her youngsters trailing after her. But it was not long before she stopped to dig up some plant bulbs and roots to eat.

The piglets stopped, too. They bumped into each other and sent up a cloud of dust. Grunting softly, they rolled in the dirt. Not for long, though. The warthog had just sighted three cheetah cubs playing under a tree a short distance away. Fearing that their mother was nearby and that she would like a piglet meal for her cubs, the warthog quickly led her family back to their burrow.

The cheetah cubs continued playing, while their mother, half-hidden under a thicket, watched for danger. She too was aware that her cubs had enemies: lions, leopards, hyenas and other predators.

Presently the cheetah came out in the open. She was a big cat, slightly smaller than the leopard, and she had a tawny black-spotted coat. Her long body and slender legs made it possible for her to run faster than any land animal.

She sat down with her front legs help upright in front of her the way a dog sits. Her feet were also similar to those of a dog. They had hard pads and claws that were wonderful for moving fast, and helped her to make sudden stops and turns.

The cheetah began to groom herself. She ran her tongue along her beautiful fur, washing her long slender legs and long tail. After that, she carefully scanned the horizon, her amber-colored eyes taking in everything.

It was not long before she saw six Bohor reedbucks grazing a short distance away. They were medium-size antelope, related to the waterbucks, or marsh antelope. The cheetah started walking slowly toward them when suddenly one of the group saw her and whistled shrilly to warn the others. With tails pressed down between their legs, they bounded off to get a head start.

The cheetah raced after them, her long legs moving like streaks of lightning. But since she could run only a short distance at a great speed, the reedbucks escaped.

After catching her breath, the cheetah returned to her waiting cubs. They did not seem to mind that she had not succeeded in hunting a meal for them. It had happened before.

A short while later the cheetah raced a reedbuck that did not have a head start. With her body arched and her large hind feet striking the ground, the cheetah rushed at her prey. She brought it crashing to the ground and killed it. Then she pulled the dead reedbuck to her cubs who had trailed behind her.

Immediately they began to eat the still warm meat. After they had their fill, the mother licked the face of each cub clean. Purring loudly in the manner of house cats, the cubs lay near their mother and went to sleep, while she had her share of the kill.

5 · The Zebras

Not far from where the cheetah cubs were sleeping, a pack of twelve dwarf mongooses were scurrying through the grass, hunting for food. They were weasel-like animals with dark brown and yellow coats. Each one was ten inches long from nose to rump with an eight-inch tail.

The sun beat down on the mongooses, but they did not seem to mind the heat. They were used to it. They always hunted for insects and mice in the daytime and not at night.

This afternoon, however, the hunting was not as good as usual. So one mongoose headed for a large mound of hard earth where termites, grass-eating insects, once lived. Some termite mounds are up to 40 feet high, and are home to a colony of as many as three million termites. But a large hartebeest antelope was using this old termite mound as a lookout post. He stood on top of it and watched for trespassers on his territory. Finally he saw an intruder grazing on his grounds. The hartebeest took off at a fast gallop and chased the trespasser away.

With the hartebeest gone, the mongoose squeezed its slender body through a narrow opening of the mound. Down it went into the darkness below where it found some snails to eat.

A few moments later an elephant rubbed its itching body against the mound, using it as a scratching post. Elephants often wear down old termite mounds by rubbing on them. When they do this, the fertile hard earth is returned to the soil where it nourishes new growing grasses.

The mongoose heard the elephant scratching. Frightened, it scooted out of the mound into the high grass. It watched the elephant move on. Then, seeing its enemy, a hyena, a short distance away, the mongoose darted back into the old termite mound where it felt it would be safe.

After the mongoose had eaten well, it started back to its pack. On the way it found an abandoned egg in a bird's nest on the ground. The mongoose picked up the egg and threw it backwards between its hind legs. The egg hit a stone, and the shell broke into pieces. The mongoose had a second meal and then went by some zebras who were grazing peacefully, shoulder to shoulder. It was a small herd of six mares, several young colts, and a stallion who was the head of the family. One of the mares was in foal, or pregnant.

Soon she was ready to foal, or give birth. Slowly she walked away from the herd and then lay down on the ground. In about ten minutes, a miniature zebra appeared and struggled to free his head and neck from the birth sac.

His damp white coat was marked with chocolate brown stripes that would turn darker when he was older. But the stripes were not like those of any other zebra. They were his own, just like no two people have the same fingerprints.

The mother got up and waited while her tiny foal rested. Then, bending low, she nudged him to get up on his

feet. He pushed with his front hooves and shoved with his hindquarters. Halfway up, he fell back to the ground with a thump. He tried again, and this time he managed to stand up.

His legs wobbled, but within several minutes he was able to walk steadily around his mother. He searched with his nose along her side, and soon he was drinking her warm milk, swishing his tail from side to side with pleasure.

After a while, the mother zebra led her baby back to the herd. They were grazing, but they looked up and stared at the tiny foal. Then they gathered around him.

The mother lowered her head and flattened her ears—a signal for them not to come too close to her baby. A tiny foal will follow another zebra, and she wanted her baby to know her own smell, call and stripes so that he would stay with her.

One morning the foal rolled in the dust with his mother to get rid of biting insects. But their dust bath was soon interrupted when the stallion snorted a warning. He had just seen a pack of eight African wild dogs approaching. They were not true dogs, but relatives of the hyena. They had large ears and splotchy black, white and brown coats.

The stallion and his herd immediately took off at a galloping pace, their excited bark-like cries filling the air. The wild dogs, their ears laid back and tails out straight, raced after the zebras. As they drew closer, they howled their hunting cries.

Terrified, the herd of zebras raced on, but soon they became winded and had to slow down. The wild dogs gained on them. They were ready to attack, but suddenly

they turned away and began chasing a zebra from another fleeing herd. She was an old mare who was too weak to keep up with the others. The wild dogs rushed up and killed her.

They did not fight among themselves as to who would get the biggest part of their kill. Instead, they shared the meal with each other. When they had finished eating, another member of their pack arrived. He was crippled. So the wild dogs shared the meal they had already eaten by throwing up chunks of meat for him.

By this time, the stallion and his herd were grazing a few yards away. The air was humid, and flies buzzed everywhere. The zebras slapped at the flies with their switching tails, and kept on eating—except the stallion. A rival had just arrived who wanted his mares. He was a young stallion and was willing to fight for them.

The older stallion snorted in anger and rushed at his rival. They circled each other, tossed their heads and pawed the ground. They reared and neck-wrestled, and then grabbed a mouthful of each other's manes. They lashed out with their powerful hooves.

But the older stallion was stronger. He forced his rival to the ground and tore a gash into his hide with his long yellow teeth. The young stallion, bleeding and in pain, got up and slowly walked away. The older stallion went and grazed with his mares.

6 · The Water Hole

More days slipped by. Rivers and streams had dried up on the grasslands, so the animals searched for small amounts of water in water holes.

A small flock of ostriches sprinted across the dusty surface of a dry river bed. Ostriches are the largest of all birds in the world. They are seven feet tall and weigh 350 pounds. They cannot fly, but they use their small wings for courting at mating time.

After the flock had reached the edge of the dry river bed, they stopped and ate some plants. The moisture that was left in them would satisfy their thirst for a while because ostriches can go for a long period without water.

The stallion and his herd of zebras felt differently. They moved along, ready to stop at the first water hole. At last they found one, but a hippopotamus had just lowered its huge body into it and was splashing around with only his nose above the surface. The hippo would stay there the rest

of the day, otherwise his skin would blister from the hot sun and he might die.

The zebras marched on. Finally they came to a place where a spring had bubbled to the surface and made a fine water hole. But the zebras had to wait their turn. Several antelope were leaping and kicking up their heels in the water before they would drink.

When the antelope left, three giraffes who had been waiting, trotted up to the water's edge. Spreading their long legs apart, they bent low and drank their fill. No sooner had they moved on than two enormous black rhinoceroses ambled up to the water hole.

Rhinoceroses are so near-sighted they are almost blind.

But their hearing and sense of smell is very keen. The two rhinoceroses sniffed the air for their enemy, man with his gun. Then each drank in turn while the other stood guard. After that, they plastered their hides with wet mud to protect themselves from biting insects.

As the rhinoceroses trotted off, the zebras saw their chance. The water was muddy. Just the same, they dipped their muzzles into it and drank, while the stallion stood by. He knew that a water hole was a dangerous place, that an enemy could attack his herd by surprise. Ears alert, nostrils quivering, the stallion kept looking around.

Suddenly he heard a slight noise in some bushes near the water hole. A young lion was hiding there. As he crept forward to sneak up on a zebra at the water's edge, the stallion spotted him. He snorted a warning, and his herd rushed off in a tight bunch.

The stallion faced the young lion. He bared his teeth and struck out with his forefeet. The young lion drew back. He did not want to be attacked by an angry stallion. Slowly he walked away. The stallion took a long drink, and tossed his head so that droplets splashed around his ears. Then he joined his herd.

By evening, the grazing animals had left the water holes. Many of them were settled for the night. They were no match for the sharp eyes of their enemies in the darkness. So the night shift of animals took over at the water holes. Elephants, lions, leopards, hyenas, wild dogs, jackals and bats came to satisfy their thirst.

At sunrise the next day, a troop of baboons left the treetops where they had slept for the night and began searching for a water hole. Baboons are the largest in the family of monkeys. A big male baboon was leading his group of youngsters and females with babies riding on their backs. Adult males were scattered in the center and the rear to protect the troop from enemies.

On and on the troop marched, barking and screaming loudly. When they reached a water hole, they quickly satisfied their thirst. Their leader then took them to some grass and plants. While they were eating, the faint scent of a leopard hung in the warm air. The big cat was crouched behind a jumble of rocks and tall grass.

The big baboon immediately barked the danger signal.
The troop rushed together, all except one youngster who
had scampered away and was playing with some leaves.
Terrified at being separated from the troop, he started running to catch up with them. As he came near the rocks, the
leopard sprang and grabbed him.

The big baboon saw what had happened, and hurried to
the youngster's rescue. Fearlessly, he attacked the leopard,
biting him in the neck with his long pointed teeth. The
leopard quickly let go of the youngster, and tried to throw
off the big baboon. The big baboon struck again, and this
time his sharp teeth wounded the leopard. Screaming, the
big cat moved slowly away, and the big baboon went back
to his troop with the youngster.

Several days later, the big baboon set out with his group on a journey. They were heading for an area where there would be plenty of good food and water because of heavier rainfall.

Predators and other animals were also leaving the parched grasslands. The stallion and his herd were with another herd of zebras. They traveled single file, one behind the other. They passed by trees that had dropped their

shriveled leaves and dry grass stems that were hard and tough.

Before long, the zebras and other animals noticed that large dark clouds had piled up in the sky. Streaks of lightning danced here and there. And thunder rumbled from a distance. The animals were not alarmed. They welcomed the coming storm. The rain would fill the parched water holes and make good grass sprout.

Alas, the storm did not favor the animals. It circled around them. But lightning struck, setting fire to the very dry grass. Thick columns of smoke rose into the sky and flames leaped in all directions.

Mice, lizards, and snakes quickly took refuge in holes underground and under rocks. The larger animals raced away from the roaring fire. But grasshoppers, beetles and other insects were not as fortunate. Hawks dove through the smoke, snatched them up and ate them. And small hungry birds picked up the insects that were on the fringes of the fire.

When the flames finally died out, they left hundreds of acres of scorched ground covered with a powdery black ash. It looked as if nothing would ever grow there again.

But when the rains did come, they brought new life to the blackened earth. The deep underground roots of the burnt grasses were still alive. They had stored away starchy food in their stems and roots. Now they sucked up the moisture in the soil, and soon sent up new green shoots.

The tall acacia and other trees whose branches had been beyond the reach of the flames began opening their bud leaves and showing blossoms. They had kept some moisture in their trunks and branches during the dry season, and so were still alive.

In a short time, the animals returned to the fresh grasses that covered the ground like a green carpet. Zebras, antelope and other grazing animals had plenty of good food now. Some would be killed by lions, leopards, cheetahs, hyenas and other animals. They had come back to the grasslands and would hunt them for food. But many predators and grazing animals would also be killed by humans.

7 · Protecting African Wildlife

          Each wild animal living on the African grasslands depends upon another animal or plant for food. Lions, cheetahs, hyenas, wild dogs and other predators feed on the grazing animals—zebras and antelope. If the predators did not hunt and eat these animals, they would multiply and eat all the grass. Then there would be no more food for them, and they would starve. The predators would die too because they depend on the grazing animals for their food.

          But humans have upset the food chain on the grasslands. Today, these changes are endangering the wildlife in Africa. True, the governments of the different countries have established national parks and wildlife refuges for some of the wild animals. But poachers are killing the animals in these parks. Poachers are men who hunt illegally for game and sell the meat, hides and horns. They use poisoned arrows, rifles and spears, and set wire snares in bushes. Every year, in Tanzania's Serengeti National Park alone, poachers kill about 30,000 animals, especially leopards and cheetahs because of their prized fur. One poacher killed as many as 4,000 zebras.

Poachers are also responsible for killing wild animals on grasslands outside the parks and game reserves. This is because government officials can make extra money by working together with poachers. Here is how it works:

According to the law in some African nations, hides of animals cannot be shipped out of the country without licenses to show that the animals were killed legally. Yet members of the game departments have given poachers forged export documents which say that it was all right to kill certain animals.

Thoughtless people pay big prices for leopard and cheetah fur coats, zebra hides, lionskin rugs, articles made of carved elephant tusks and powdered rhinoceros horns.

But poaching is not the only problem that exists in Africa today. Despite a recent law against sports hunting in Kenya, elephants, zebras, antelope, giraffes, lions, leopards and cheetahs are becoming scarcer. This is because of Africa's growing human population. People have taken over grasslands inhabited by wild animals for farms to grow food and for ranches to raise cattle.

As a result, many elephants have had to seek refuge in parks. Unfortunately, these animals are too big for some parks. They soon destroy large areas of vegetation and uproot thousands of trees for food. To save the trees for leopards and grass for grazing animals, elephants are being shot. The shooting reduces the number of elephants, and saves the park lands for all the animals—not just elephants.

At one time, lions ranged throughout most of Africa. Now, when lions prey on domestic cattle for food, they are killed. So the places where lions can live in the world are getting smaller and smaller.

The Transafrican Highway also poses a threat to the wildlife in Africa. This highway, which is now being built through Equatorial Africa, will run from coast to coast. Some of the highway will cut through part of the grasslands of north-central Africa. New cities and towns will spring up. Then there will be more farms and ranches, and there will be no place for the zebras, giraffes and other animals.

There is no doubt that Africa needs land to feed its growing human population. But even the national parks are in danger of becoming smaller to make room for human settlements and farms. Let us hope that in the future the African governments will not decrease the size of parks. Let us also hope that they will save some grasslands outside these areas for the wild animals, and that they will enforce stricter laws and prison terms for poachers. Then the dwindling number of wild animals will eventually increase.

The wildlife that exists in Africa is a priceless heritage. It should be preserved, otherwise the day might come when we will only see the wild animals of Africa in zoos.

Index

L

Laurasia, 7
leopards, 10, 26, 27, 28, 30, 34,
    50, 52, 53, 58, 59, 60, 61
lionesses, 11, 12, 13, 14, 15, 16,
    18, 19, 23
lions, 10, 11, 13, 14, 15, 18, 20,
    28, 29, 30, 34, 50, 58, 59, 61,
    62; lionskin, 60
lizards, 56

M

mares, 41, 45, 46
mice, 39, 56
mongooses, 39, 41
mouse, 27

O

ostriches, 47, 48
owl, 27

P

Pangaea, 7
Panthalassa, 7
piglets, 31, 33
poachers, 59, 60, 61, 62
predators, 10, 14, 20, 34, 54, 58,
    59
pregnant, 41
pride of lions, 11, 20, 23, 26
puff adder snake, 32, 33

R

rhinoceroses, 60; black, 9, 10, 49,
    50

S

Sahara desert, 10
secretary bird, 32, 33
Serengeti National Park, 59
snakes, 32, 56
South America, 7
stallion, 41, 44, 45, 46, 48, 50, 54
symbiosis, 24

T

Tanzania, 59
territory, 14, 21, 22, 26, 39
termites, 39; termite mounds, 39,
    41
Transafrican Highway, 62

V

vultures, 23

W

water holes, 47, 48, 49, 50, 52,
    55
warthogs, 10, 31, 32, 33
wild dogs, 10, 44, 45, 50, 59

Z

zebras, 10, 13, 24, 31, 41, 42, 43,
    44, 45, 48, 49, 50, 54, 55, 58,
    59, 60, 61, 62